PRIMARY PARTNERS

A- Z Activities
to Make Learning Fun
for Nursery and Age 3
(SUNBEAM NURSERY)

Jane Banks

Fun-to-Make Visuals ◘ Copy-and-Create Crafts

Simple Supplies Needed ◘ Matching Thought Treats

W9-AHU-586

SUPPLEMENTAL MATERIAL FOR PRIMARY LESSONS

AND FAMILY HOME EVENING USE

to Reinforce Gospel Topics

You'll Find: A-Z Topics to Match Primary Lessons

Adam   Animals   Birds & Insects   Body   Brothers & Sisters
Child   Church   Day & Night   Ears   Easter   Example   Eyes
Family   Feelings   Fish & Water Animals   Food & Clothing
Forgive   Friends   Hands   Helping   Holy Ghost   Home
Honesty   Jesus Was Born   Jesus   Love   Love Others   Music
Obedience   Plan   Prayer   Prophet   Reverence   Sabbath Day
Sacrament   Scriptures   Smell & Taste   Sorry   Things
Trees, Plants & Flowers   Water

Covenant Communications, Inc.
American Fork, Utah

Printed in the United States of America
First Printing: April 1995

95 96 97 98 99 00   10 9 8 7 6 5 4 3 2 1

Primary Partners: A-Z Activities to Make Learning Fun!
ISBN 1-55503-809-3

INTRODUCTION

PRIMARY PARTNERS:
A-Z Activities to Make Learning Fun
for Nursery and Age 3
(SUNBEAM NURSERY)

Children and parents alike will love the easy, fun-to-create visuals contained in this volume. Patterns for each of the projects are actual size, ready to Copy-n-Create in minutes. You'll enjoy using many of the Primary Partners crafts and activities to supplement your Primary 1* lessons, enhance your family home evenings, and help children learn gospel principles in fun, creative ways.

HOW TO USE THIS BOOK

1. <u>Preview A-Z Table of Contents</u> to find pictures and subjects.
2. <u>Use Lesson Cross Reference Index</u> on page iv. Match your lesson number with the A-Z subject to find activities quickly.
3. <u>Shop Ahead For Simple Supplies</u>. Each activity requires a few basic items: Copies of patterns, scissors, tape, glue, crayons, zip-close plastic bags, paper punch, yarn or ribbon, wooden craft sticks, velcro or safety pins, double stick tape, fabric pieces, plastic sheets, and paper grocery sacks.
4. <u>Copy Patterns Ahead</u>. You'll save time and avoid last minute preparation.
5. <u>Organize Activities</u> in an A-Z file. Copy instructions to include with the pattern copies and supplies.
6. <u>Send Home a Show-and-Tell Sack.</u> The first week, decorate a sack that each child can take home to display creations. Attach a note (found on page ii) that reads:

   "Dear Parents, This is your child's Sunny SUNDAY Sack. Each week, please help your child display Primary or family home evening creations. Self-esteem builds as items are shown and lessons retold. Place creations in the show-and-tell pocket during the week to reinforce the gospel topic. Then, when next week's creation appears, <u>store past project in the sack</u>."

TO MAKE SACK: Copy sun and glue-on sticker patterns on pages ii and iii on cardstock paper. Glue stickers and sunshine pieces on a large grocery sack, gluing bottom piece only 1/4" on sides and bottom (leaving top open to create a pocket).

*Primary 1 manual is published by The Church of Jesus Christ of Latter-day Saints, Salt Lake City, Utah.

Dear Parents:
This is:

_____'s
**Sunny
SUNDAY Sack**.
Each week,
please help your
child display Primary
or family home
evening creations.
Self-esteem
builds as items are
shown and lessons
retold.
Place creations in
the show-and-tell
pocket during the
week to reinforce the
gospel topic. Then,
when next week's
creation appears,
store past project in
the sack.

Thank you.

_____
Primary Teacher

PATTERN: Sunny SUNDAY Sack pocket and glue-on stickers

There is shine in my heart.

I am a Child of God!

I am a Child of God!

Show-and-Tell Pocket

My Heavenly Father loves me!

SUNDAY is a special day!

LESSON CROSS REFERENCE INDEX to Primary 1 manual*

*Primary 1 manual is published by the Church of Jesus Christ of Latter-day Saints, Salt Lake City, Utah.

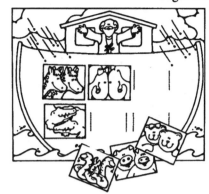
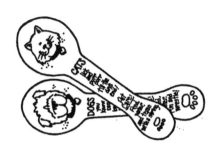

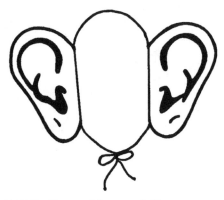

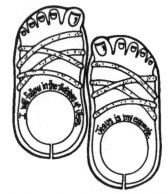

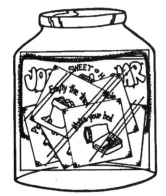

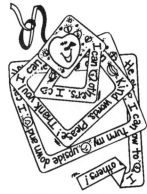

PRAY: To Heavenly Father I Will Pray (Daniel & lions' drama scene) . . . 66-67

PRAYER: I Like to Pray with My Family (family prayer fan) 66, 68

PROPHET: I Know the Prophet Lives (prophet poster fold-out pictures)   69-70

REVERENCE Begins With Me (church mouse maze) 69, 71

SABBATH DAY: Sunday Is My Best Day (creation collar) 72-74

SACRAMENT: I Like to Remember Jesus (manners match game) 72, 75

SCRIPTURES From Heavenly Father and Jesus (scripture specs) 76-77

SMELL & TASTE: I Am Thankful For (giant nose and tongue mask) 76, 78

SORRY: I Can Say Hippopotamus and I'm Sorry. (hippo sack puppet) . . 79-80

THINGS: I Can Do Many Things (shirt with buttons sewing card) 79, 81

TREES, PLANTS, & FLOWERS: Creator's Garden (bracelets) 82-83

WATER: It's a Wonder (umbrella with raindrop glue-on stickers) 82, 84

A

ADAM: Adam and Eve in Heavenly Father's Image

(paper doll pleats)

See lesson #14 in Primary 1 manual*.

YOU'LL NEED: Copy of sign and paper doll patterns (page 2) on colored cardstock paper, one 8 1/2" x 11" sheet of lightweight paper for each child, scissors, glue, and crayons

ACTIVITY: Create paper doll pleats to show that Adam and Eve look like Heavenly Father.
TO CREATE PLEATS & SIGN:
1. Measure 1 1/4" on edge of an 8 1/2" x 11" paper. Fan-fold six folds.
2. Trace paper doll pattern on top fold and cut out shape to find three connecting images.
3. Glue paper doll pleats in place below sign.
4. Draw in faces and hair, and color.

THOUGHT TREAT: Gingerbread girl and boy

ANIMALS: I'm Thankful for Animals--They Help Me

(picture with glue-on stickers)

See lesson #12 in Primary 1 manual*.
See next activity for more ideas on lesson #12.

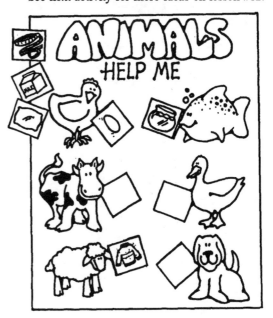

YOU'LL NEED: Copy of picture and glue-on matching sticker patterns (page 3) on colored cardstock paper for each child, scissors, glue, and crayons

ACTIVITY: Match the animals with glue-on stickers to show how animals help us with food and clothing, and they are fun to have for pets.
1. Color and cut out picture and glue-on stickers.
2. Glue stickers on next to matching animals, birds, and fish.

THOUGHT TREAT:
Animal cookies or crackers

PATTERN: Adam, Eve, and Heavenly Father (paper doll pleats and sign)   See lesson #14 in Primary 1 manual*.

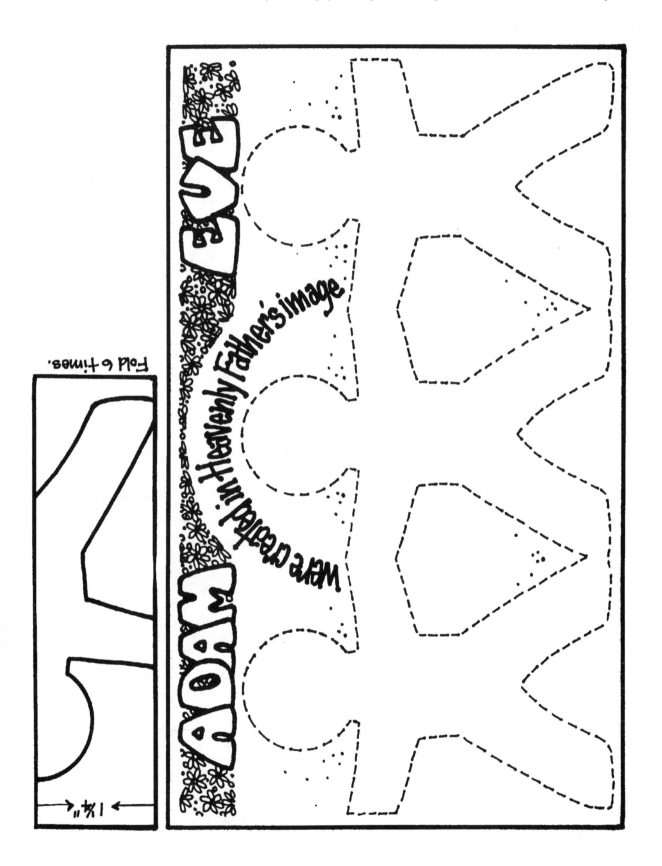

Fold 6 times.

1¾"

EVE

ADAM

were created in Heavenly Father's image.

  *Primary 1 manual is published by The Church of Jesus Christ of Latter-day Saints, Salt Lake City, Utah.

PATTERN: ANIMALS (picture with matching glue on stickers)   See lesson #12 in Primary 1 manual*.

A

ANIMALS: I'm Thankful For Animals Saved From the Flood

(Noah's ark with 3-D animal tabs)

See lesson #12 in Primary 1 manual*.
See previous activity for more ideas on lesson #12.

YOU'LL NEED: Copy of ark and animal tab patterns (pages 5-6) on colored cardstock paper for each child, scissors, razor blade (to use prior to activity), and crayons

ACTIVITY: Act out saving animals from the flood by placing animals in slots.
1. Before activity, cut out slits in ark with a razor blade or the X-ACTO® number one knife.
2. Child colors ark and animal tabs.
3. Cut out animal tabs and insert tabs into slits. Animals will bend in "U" shape to produce a 3-D effect.

THOUGHT TREAT: Animal cookies or crackers

ANIMALS: I Can Be Kind to Animals

(cat and dog spoon)

See lesson #35 in Primary 1 manual*.

YOU'LL NEED: Copy of dog and cat spoon pattern (page 7) on colored cardstock paper, for each child, OPTION: A regular dog bone biscuit and 12" of yarn or ribbon, scissors, glue, and crayons

ACTIVITY: Create a cat and dog spoon to show ways they can take care of their pets.
1. Cut out and color dog and cat spoon.
2. Glue back to back.
FUN OPTION: Tie a regular dog bone biscuit around the middle of spoon and tell child to take it home to feed their dog or ask a friend's parents if you can give it to their dog.   Note: Dog Bone Cookie recipe below is too sweet for dogs.

THOUGHT TREAT: Dog Bone Cookie
1. Roll and cut out sugar cookie or gingerbread dough into dog bone shapes (pattern on page 7).
2. Bake at 350° for 8-10 minutes.
3. Tell child not to feed dog bone cookies to their dogs, because pets should not eat sweets.

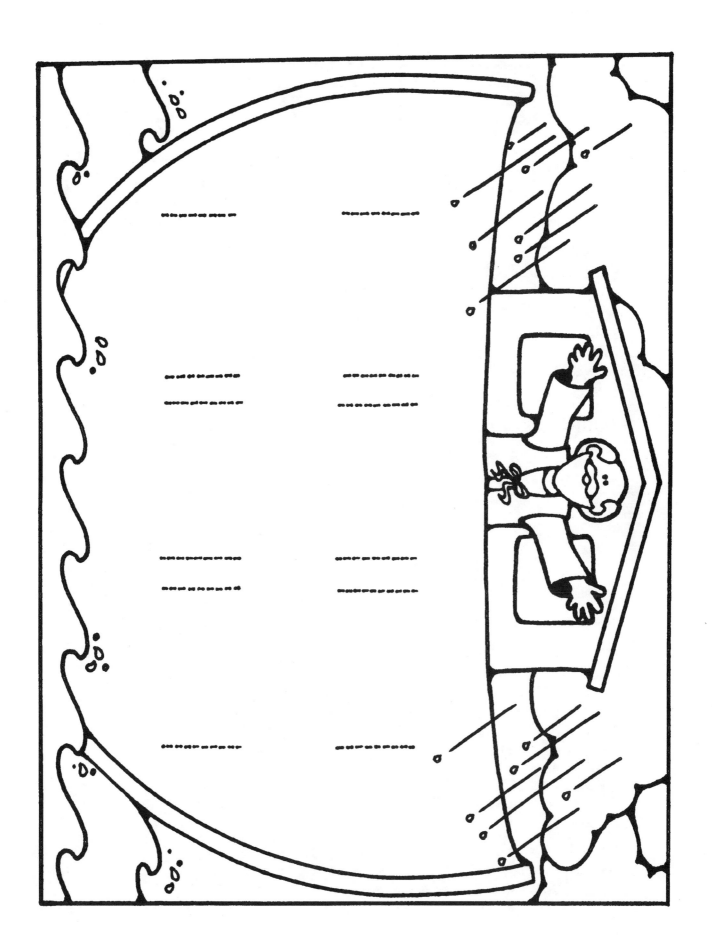

*Primary 1 manual is published by The Church of Jesus Christ of Latter-day Saints, Salt Lake City, Utah.

PATTERN: ANIMALS (cat and dog spoon)

See lesson #35 in Primary 1 manual*.

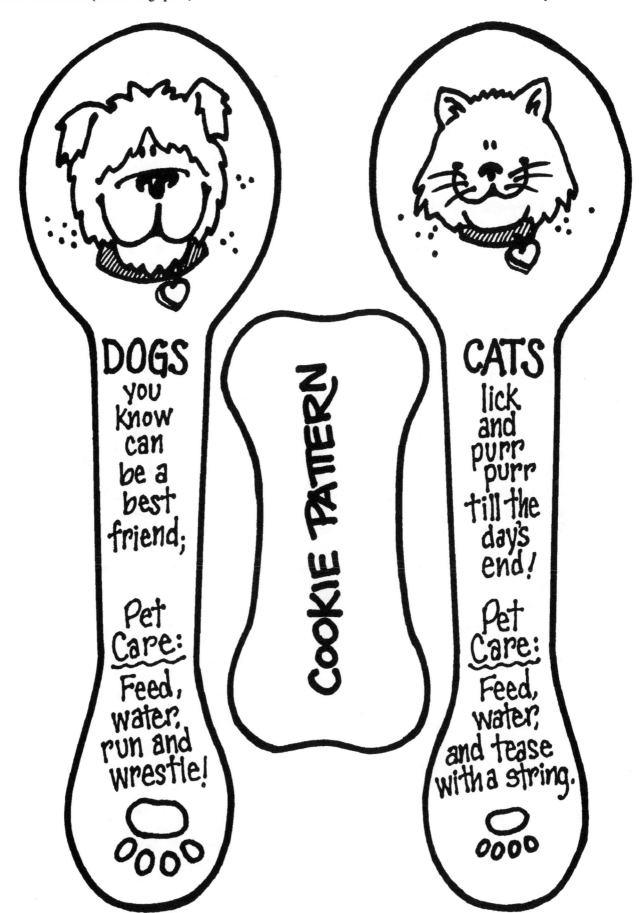

DOGS
you
know
can
be a
best
friend;

Pet
Care:
Feed,
water,
run and
wrestle!

COOKIE PATTERN

CATS
lick
and
purr
purr
till the
day's
end!

Pet
Care:
Feed,
water,
and tease
with a string.

*Primary 1 manual is published by The Church of Jesus Christ of Latter-day Saints, Salt Lake City, Utah.

B

BIRDS & INSECTS: I'm Thankful For

(bird watch, bug jar, and/or "nature walk" binoculars)   See lesson #13 in Primary 1 manual*.

YOU'LL NEED: Copy of bird watch, insects, bug jar, and/or "Nature Walk" binocular patterns (pages 9-12) on colored cardstock paper, scissors, glue, and crayons. PLUS:
o BIRD WATCH: Safety pin, tape, or "sticky-back" velcro to attach watch to child's wrist
o BUG JAR: Zip-close plastic sandwich bag for each child
o BINOCULARS: Yarn or ribbon (40" for each child) and paper punch

ACTIVITY CHOICES:

o SEAGULL BIRD WATCH: Illustrating the seagulls that helped save the pioneers from the crickets.
1. Color and cut out bird watch and wristband.
2. Glue bird on wristband.
3. Tape or pin bird watch to wrist with a safety pin, or attach with "sticky-back" velcro.

o BUG JAR: If making a bird watch and bug jar, pull out cricket and pretend to have bird eat cricket to tell the pioneer story.
1. Color and cut out bug jar and insect pictures.
2. Attach plastic bag to jar with double stick tape.
3. Enclose bugs in plastic bag.

o NATURE WALK BINOCULARS: With these giant binoculars around their neck, children really want to look at Heavenly Father's creations. Take a walk around outside the meetinghouse to see what you can see: Bugs, insects, birds, trees, plants, flowers, and little people.

1. Color and cut out binoculars.
2. Punch holes at top.
3. Tape binoculars together.
4. Tie yarn or ribbon through holes and place around child's neck.

THOUGHT TREATS: Sunflower seeds that birds eat, or candy gummy worms, and/or tiny sandwiches to take on nature hike

PATTERN: BIRDS & INSECTS (bird watch)   See lesson #13 in Primary 1 manual*.

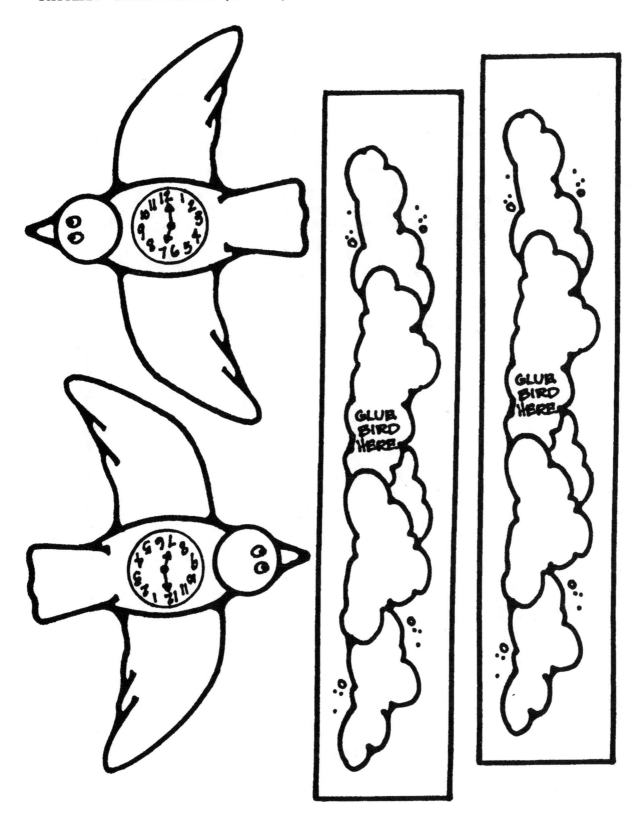

GLUE
BIRD
HERE

GLUE
BIRD
HERE

MY BUG JAR

ATTACH PLASTIC BAG HERE

*Primary 1 manual is published by The Church of Jesus Christ of Latter-day Saints, Salt Lake City, Utah.

PATTERN: BIRDS & INSECTS (bugs to enclose in bug jar)   See lesson #13 in Primary 1 manual*.

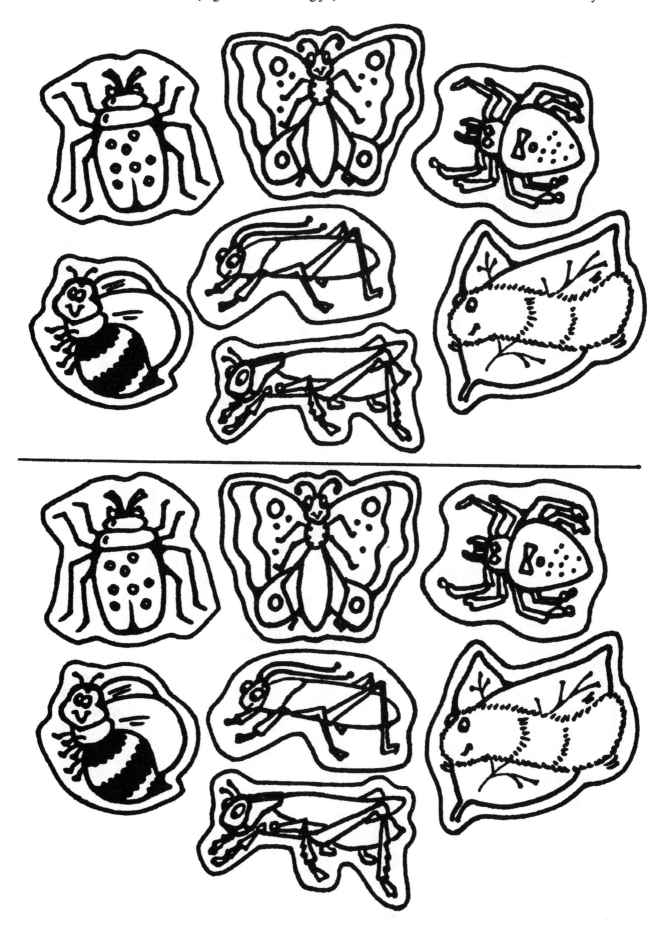

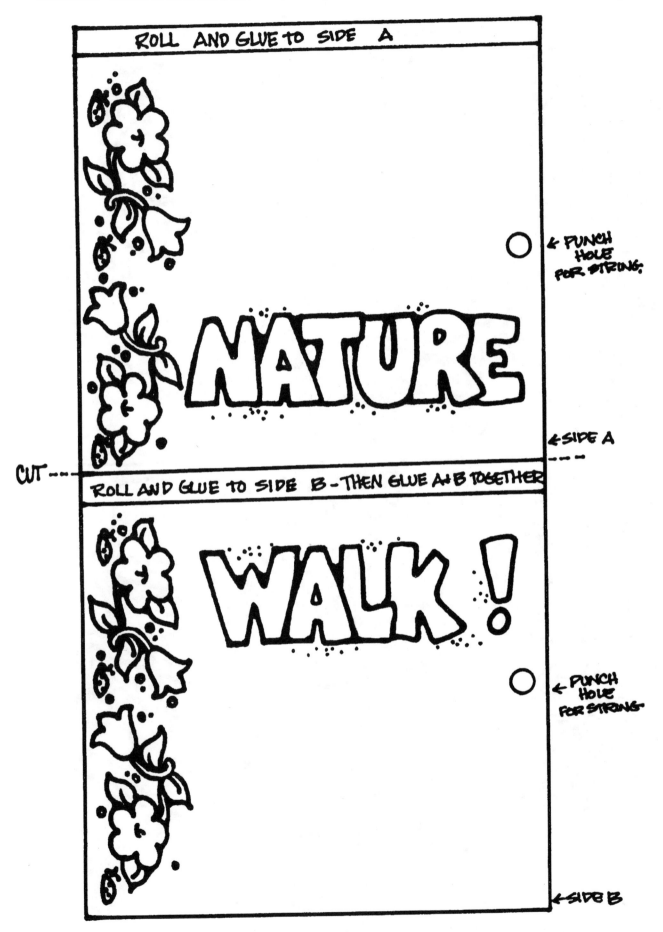

*Primary 1 manual is published by The Church of Jesus Christ of Latter-day Saints, Salt Lake City, Utah.

B

BODY: My Body Is Special

(body puzzle or hinges doll)

See lesson #16 in Primary 1 manual*.

YOU'LL NEED: Copy of body pattern (page 14) on cardstock paper for each child, scissors, glue, crayons, and the following -- choose from two options:
♥ #1 BODY BUILDING PUZZLE:
8 1/2" x 11" cardstock paper for each child
♥ #2 HINGES DOLL:
Five brads for each doll

ACTIVITY: Create a body building picture or hinges doll to show that the body is special.
♥ OPTION #1--Body Building Puzzle: Color and cut out doll puzzle. Glue body parts to body on an 8 1/2" x 11" piece of cardstock paper.
♥ OPTION #2--Hinges Doll: If you don't have cardstock paper, glue/mount doll on construction paper. Color and cut out body pieces and attach to the body with brads to make parts moveable.

THOUGHT TREAT: Gingerbread girl or boy

BODY: My Body Looks Like Heavenly Father and Jesus

(look-alike two-sided puzzle)

See lesson #2 in Primary 1 manual*.

YOU'LL NEED: Copy of two-sided puzzle pattern (page 15) on cardstock paper, an envelope or zip-close plastic sandwich bag to store puzzle pieces for each child, scissors, glue, and crayons

ACTIVITY: Create a two-sided puzzle with Heavenly Father and Jesus on one side, and children on the other side to show that we are created in their image.
1. Color pictures.
2. Fold pictures in half on dividing line back-to-back.
3. Glue pictures together (spreading glue over the entire piece, not just the edges).
4. Trim edges. Cut puzzle shapes out as shown on one side (into six pieces).
5. Place puzzle in an envelope or plastic bag for child to take home.

THOUGHT TREAT: Sugar cookie girl and boy (color clothes with frosting or paint cookie dough before baking). Cookie Paints: Mix two teaspoons canned milk with food coloring.

My Body is Special!!

*Primary 1 manual is published by The Church of Jesus Christ of Latter-day Saints, Salt Lake City, Utah.

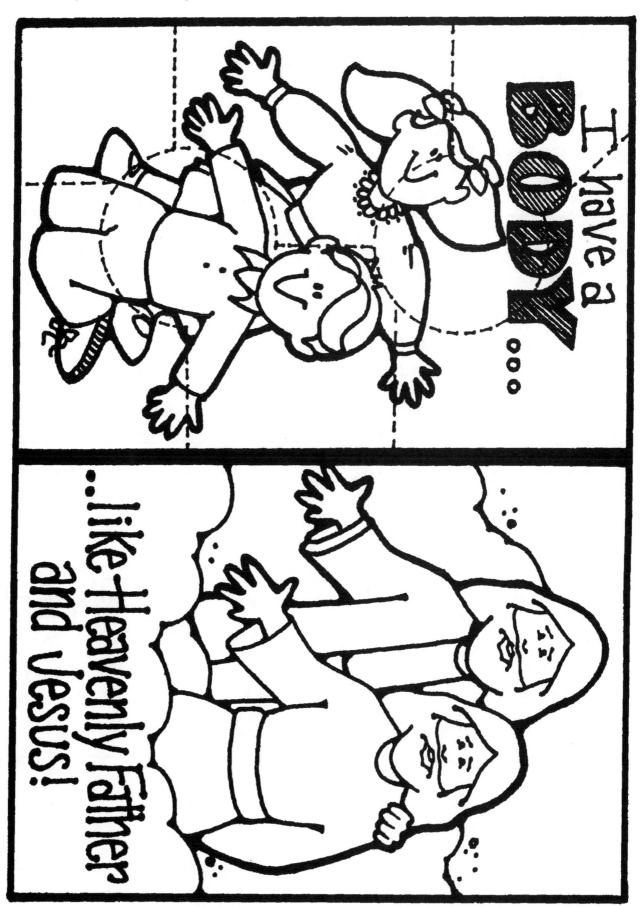

B-C

BROTHERS & SISTERS: I Love You

(baby in a blanket with baby care items)

See lesson #24 in Primary 1 manual*.

YOU'LL NEED: Copy of baby, baby care items (pages 17-18) on colored cardstock paper for each child, scissors, and crayons

ACTIVITY: Create a baby in a blanket with baby items to show that baby brother or sister needs care.
1. Cut out blanket, baby and baby care items.
2. Fold blanket on fold lines and glue sides 1/4" to create a pocket for baby and baby care items.
3. Place baby and baby items in the blanket to show and talk about baby care.

THOUGHT TREAT: Baby rattle cookie, candy pacifier, or Baby in Blanket. (Wrap breadstick dough around a hotdog cut in half, leaving round end of hotdog showing. Bake at 350° for 20-25 minutes or until golden brown.)

CHILD: I Am a Child of God

(paper dolls)

See lesson #1 in Primary 1 manual*.

YOU'LL NEED: Copy of boy or girl paper doll set (pages 19-20) on colored cardstock paper for each child, scissors, and crayons

ACTIVITY: Create paper dolls to remind each child they are a spirit child of our Heavenly Father.
1. Color and cut out a girl or boy paper doll with matching clothes.
2. Fold flaps down on clothes to hold them on the doll.

THOUGHT TREAT:
Gingerbread or sugar cookie boy or girl (color clothes with colored frosting or paint cookie dough before baking. Cookie Paints: Mix two teaspoons canned milk with food coloring.

*Primary 1 manual is published by The Church of Jesus Christ of Latter-day Saints, Salt Lake City, Utah.

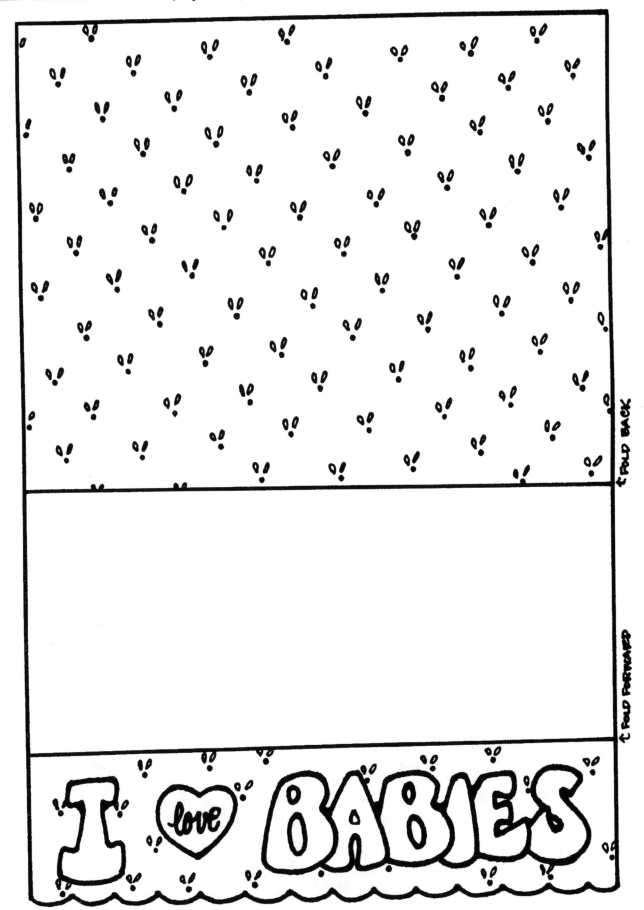

See lesson #24 in Primary 1 manual*.

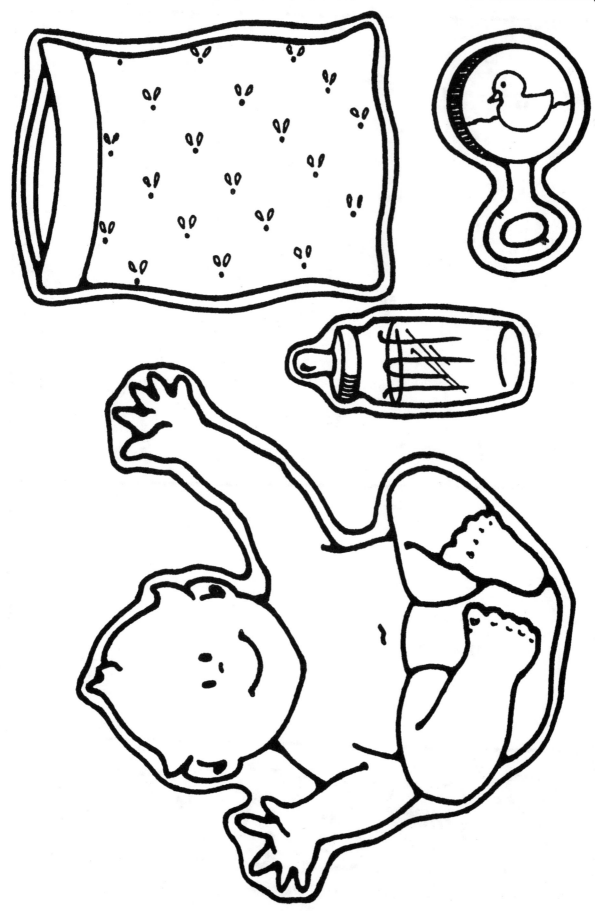

*Primary 1 manual is published by The Church of Jesus Christ of Latter-day Saints, Salt Lake City, Utah.

　　　*Primary 1 manual is published by The Church of Jesus Christ of Latter-day Saints, Salt Lake City, Utah.

C-D

CHURCH: The Church of Jesus Christ of Latter-day Saints

(name badge)   See lesson #42 in Primary 1 manual*.

YOU'LL NEED: Copy of name badge pattern
(page 22) on cardstock paper for each child, safety pin,
scissors, and crayons

ACTIVITY: Create a name badge to show that you
are part of Jesus' church.
1. Color and cut out badge.
2. Write child's name on badge.
3. Safety pin badge on child to wear with pride.

THOUGHT TREATS:
#1 Meeting Mints (tell child that Jesus "mint" them to be member of his church)
#2 Church House Cookies: Church house shaped sugar or gingerbread cookies
(pattern on page 22)

DAY & NIGHT: I Give Thanks

(window wheel)   See lesson #8 in Primary 1 manual*.

YOU'LL NEED: Copy of window wheel
patterns (pages 23-24) on cardstock paper,
a metal or button brad for each child,
scissors, and crayons

ACTIVITY: Create a day and night
window wheel to show how Heavenly
Father divided the day and the night for us
to work, play, and rest.
1. Color and cut out window wheels.
2. Cut out window on part A.
3. Attach part A on top of part B with a
metal brad or button brad (placed in
center).

TO MAKE BUTTON BRAD:
Sew two buttons together on opposite sides
(threading thread through the same hole) to
attach window wheels.

THOUGHT TREAT: Sun, moon, and star shaped cut-out cookies

     *Primary 1 manual is published by The Church of Jesus Christ of Latter-day Saints, Salt Lake City, Utah.

Push brad through center mark (✽).

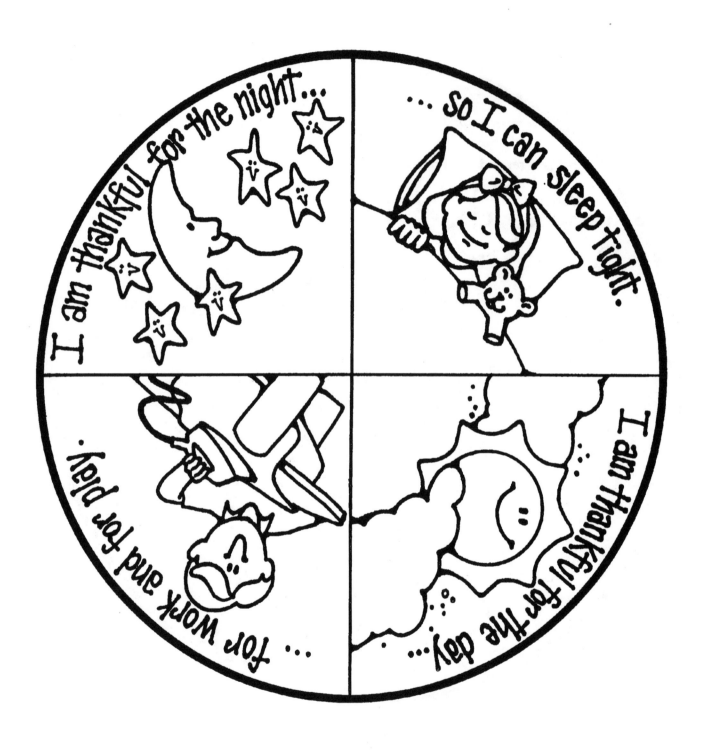

     *Primary 1 manual is published by The Church of Jesus Christ of Latter-day Saints, Salt Lake City, Utah.

E

EARS: Ears to Listen and Obey

(ear-wings)

See lesson #18 in Primary 1 manual*.

YOU'LL NEED: Copy of ear-wing pattern (page 26) on cardstock paper, 40" of yarn or ribbon for each child, scissors, glue tape, and crayons. OPTION: Copy ear-wings on flesh-colored cardstock

ACTIVITY: Ear-wings remind child to listen and obey.
1. Color and cut out ears.
2. Fold flap over ribbon, glue, and then tape to reinforce.
3. Tie around child's head under chin (over their own ears).
LISTENING FUN: While they are wearing their ears, play some music and ask them to do things to see if they can listen and obey.

THOUGHT TREAT: Face decorated cookie with large gumdrop ears

EASTER: Jesus Was Resurrected

(3-D flower garden)

See lesson #45 in Primary 1 manual*.

YOU'LL NEED: Copy of 3-D flower garden pattern (page 27) on white cardstock paper for each child, scissors, glue, and crayons

ACTIVITY: Create a 3-D flower garden to show the meaning of Easter.
Flower #1: "Jesus loves me."
Flower #2: "Jesus died for me and was resurrected."
Flower #3: "I will live again like Jesus."
1. Color and cut out spring flowers and "Easter" sign.
2. Bend petals forward on flowers to create a 3-D effect.
3. Glue flowers in place.

THOUGHT TREAT: Flower-shaped sugar cookies FUN SANDWICH: Make a sandwich with two flower shaped cookies with frosting in between. Place a gumdrop in the center.

 *Primary 1 manual is published by The Church of Jesus Christ of Latter-day Saints, Salt Lake City, Utah.

See lesson #45 in Primary 1 manual*.

*Primary 1 manual is published by The Church of Jesus Christ of Latter-day Saints, Salt Lake City, Utah.

E

EXAMPLE: Be an Example for Others

(follow Jesus sandals)

See lesson #36 in Primary 1 manual*.

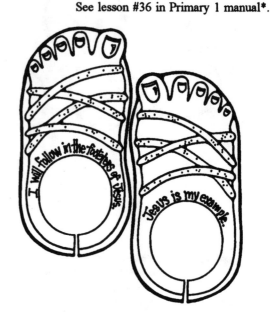

YOU'LL NEED: Copy of sandal pattern (page 29) on flesh-colored cardstock paper for each child, masking tape, scissors, and crayons

ACTIVITY: Create example sandals for child to wear over shoes, around ankle.
1. Color and cut out sandal.
2. Place around child's ankle, and tape to toe of shoe with masking tape.

THOUGHT TREAT: Footprint Cookie: Roll sugar cookie dough into two-inch balls. Make imprint in dough with side of fist. Then press down with fingers at the top to make toes. To Color Toenails: Mix food coloring with sugar in bottle and shake well. Sprinkle on toes, or mix one teaspoon canned milk with food coloring and paint toes. Bake at 350° for 8-10 minutes.

EYES: My Eyes Help Me to See

(giant eyes headband)

See lesson #19 in Primary 1 manual*.

YOU'LL NEED: Copy of giant eyes headband pattern (page 30) on cardstock paper for each child, scissors, glue, tape, and crayons

ACTIVITY: Create a headband with large eyes to remind children that their eyes help them to see many things: Colors, clouds, trees, flowers, bugs, and birds.
1. Color and cut out headband.
2. Fit headband to child's forehead and tape together.

THOUGHT TREAT: Soda crackers with olive eyes and cheese eyelashes TO MAKE: Cut an olive in half. Using squeezeable cheese, squirt a little cheese in center of cracker and press half an olive into cheese for eye. Then squirt strips of cheese around olive to make eye lashes.

   *Primary 1 manual is published by The Church of Jesus Christ of Latter-day Saints, Salt Lake City, Utah.

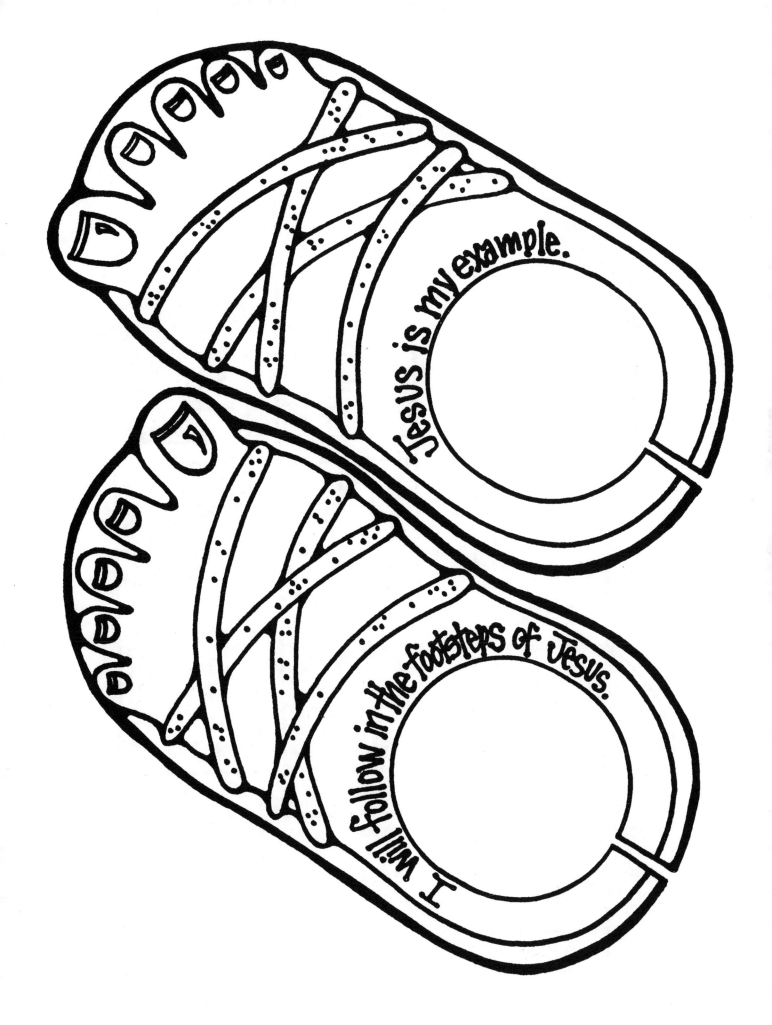

PATTERN: EYES (giant eyes headband)

See lesson #19 in Primary 1 manual*.

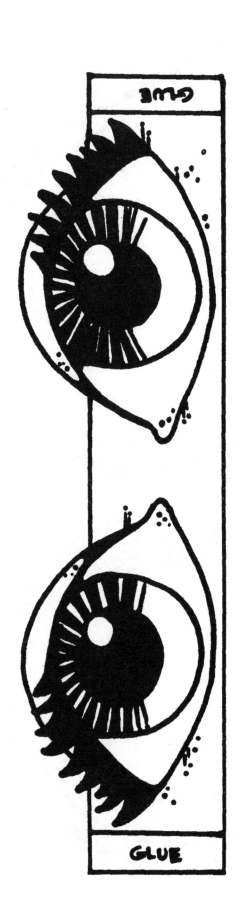

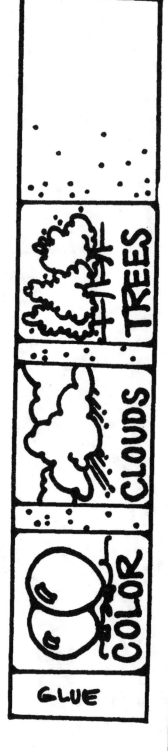

TREES

CLOUDS

COLOR

GLUE

BIRDS

BUGS

FLOWERS

GLUE

GLUE

GLUE

*Primary 1 manual is published by The Church of Jesus Christ of Latter-day Saints, Salt Lake City, Utah.

FAMILY: I Am Part of a Family

(family face block and game)   See lesson #23 in Primary 1 manual*.

YOU'LL NEED: Copy of block and glue-on sticker girl or boy face patterns (page 32) on cardstock paper for each child, scissors, glue, and crayons

ACTIVITY: Create a family face block to show children they are part of a family.
TO MAKE:
1. Color and cut out block and girl or boy glue-on sticker.
2. Glue on girl or boy in square provided.
3. Fold and glue edges, and tape down lid.
TO PLAY GAME: Have children take turns rolling block and telling something about a member of his/her family as the family member appears on the block (face up). Ideas: Tell what that family member has taught you, why you love them, or how you can help and show love to that person. When child rolls "I Am Part of a Family," he/she says, "I Love My Family."

THOUGHT TREAT: Pretzel Family Necklace: String pretzels on yarn or ribbon for child to wear home. As they eat this yummy treat, they'll think, "My family's really neat!"

FAMILY: I Love You

(family tree with glue-on stickers)   See lesson #25 in Primary 1 manual*.

YOU'LL NEED: Copy of Family "I Love You" tree and face patterns (page 33) on cardstock paper for each child, scissors, glue, and crayons

ACTIVITY: Create a family tree with glue-on sticker faces to glue on each branch. We can say "I Love You" to each family member on our tree. A way to say "I Love You" is to do kind things and say kind words. Show your teacher you love her or him by being reverent in class and in Primary.
1. Color family tree.
2. Color and cut out family faces and glue in place on family tree.
3. Have child draw their own face and hair.

THOUGHT TREAT: Heart-shaped cookie, frosted with a smiling face

Brothers & Sisters

Grandma & Grandpa

Mother

Me!

Father

I am part of a FAMILY

Me!

place boy or girl here and copy.

 *Primary 1 manual is published by The Church of Jesus Christ of Latter-day Saints, Salt Lake City, Utah.

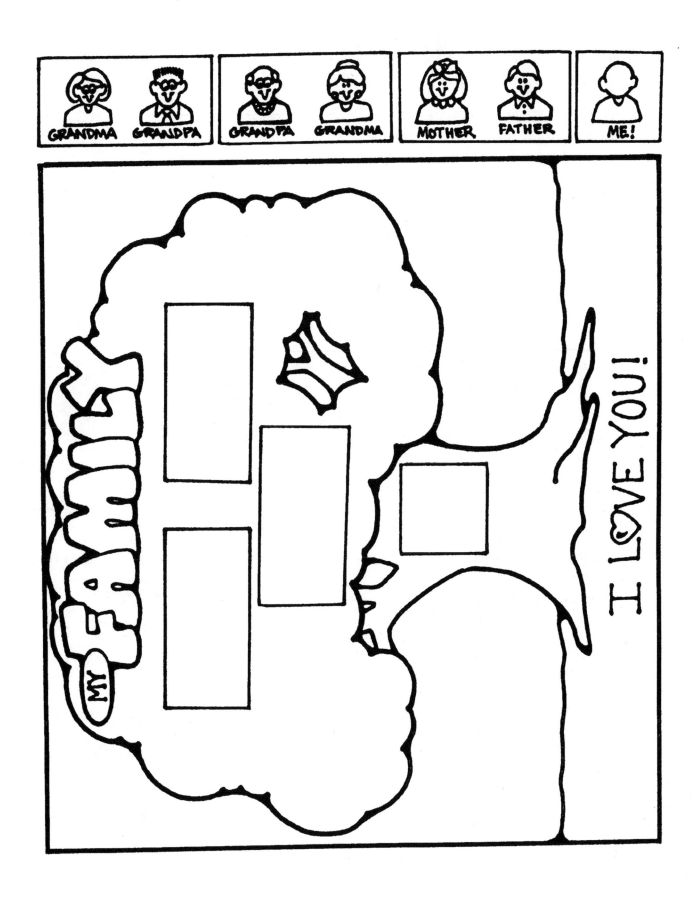

F

FAMILY: Together Forever

(temple tie and tithing purse)   See lesson #26 in Primary 1 manual*.

YOU'LL NEED: Copy of temple tie and tithing purse and coin patterns (pages 35-36) on cardstock paper for each child, scissors, glue, paper punch, yarn or ribbon, and crayons

ACTIVITY: Create a tithing purse and a temple tie for each child to learn how families can prepare to go to the temple.
TEMPLE TIE: Color and cut out tie. Punch two holes at the top and tie yarn through holes. Tie loosely around child's neck.
TITHING PURSE:
1. Color and cut out tithing purse.
2. Fold purse in half.
3. Glue together on sides and bottom, leaving top open.
4. Punch two holes on the top sides.
5. Tie yarn or ribbon through the holes at each end.
6. Cut out coins and place in purse.

THOUGHT TREAT: Money candies wrapped in gold foil, or temple mints (Tell children that Heavenly Father "mint" for you to go to the temple.)

FEELINGS: My Sunshine Face

(smile and frown flip-flag)   See lesson #21 in Primary 1 manual*.

YOU'LL NEED: Copy of smile and frown flag pattern (page 26) on cardstock paper, and a wooden craft stick (or unsharpened pencil) for each child, scissors, glue, and crayons

ACTIVITY: Create a smile and frown flip-flag. Child can learn about their feelings and know that it's more fun to have a sunshine face. To flip the flag, move it fast back and forth to try and see both sides at once.
1. Color and cut out flag.
2. Glue a wooden stick in the bottom center.
3. Fold flag and glue back to back.

THOUGHT TREAT: Smile Face Cookies

I earn a dime
My world is fine.
I pay a penny
My blessings are many!

I can pay Tithing.

*Primary 1 manual is published by The Church of Jesus Christ of Latter-day Saints, Salt Lake City, Utah.

F

FISH & WATER ANIMALS: Fishy Fun

(fish, fish bowl, and pole)

See lesson #11 in Primary 1 manual*.

YOU'LL NEED: Copy of fish, fish bowl, fishing pole, and fish hook patterns (pages 38-39) on colored cardstock paper, wooden craft stick, metal paper clips, small magnet, 12" of string, and a zip-close plastic sandwich bag for each child, scissors, double-stick tape, and crayons

ACTIVITY: Create fish and water animals, fish bowl and pole. THEN GO FISH!

1. Color and cut out fish/water animals, and bowl.
2. Using double-stick tape, attach plastic bag to fish bowl to enclose fish.
3. Attach a metal paper clip to each fish (so magnet fish hook can pull them out).
4. Place fish in bag/fish bowl.
5. Color and cut out fishing pole. Fold pattern in half and glue over wooden craft stick, poke a hole in end, and tie a string to pole.
6. Color and cut out fish hook and tie it to the other end of string. Glue a magnet on fish hook (**ahead of time** to dry).

THOUGHT TREATS: Candy gummy fish or fish-shaped crackers to place in fish bowl bag

FOOD & CLOTHING: I'm Thankful For

(food and clothing stand-up card)

See lesson #32 in Primary 1 manual*.

YOU'LL NEED: Copy of closet and cupboard card and food and clothing glue-on sticker patterns (pages 40-41) on tan cardstock paper for each child, scissors, glue, and crayons

ACTIVITY: To help child express gratitude for food and clothing, help them match up and glue food and clothing stickers to cupboard and closet.

1. Color and cut out cupboard and closet stand-up card and glue-on stickers.
2. Fold card in the middle.
3. Match up food and clothing stickers to their right places in the cupboard and closet.

THOUGHT TREAT: Food (Before eating, have a child thank Heavenly Father for the food and clothing and ask him to bless the food.)

 *Primary 1 manual is published by The Church of Jesus Christ of Latter-day Saints, Salt Lake City, Utah.

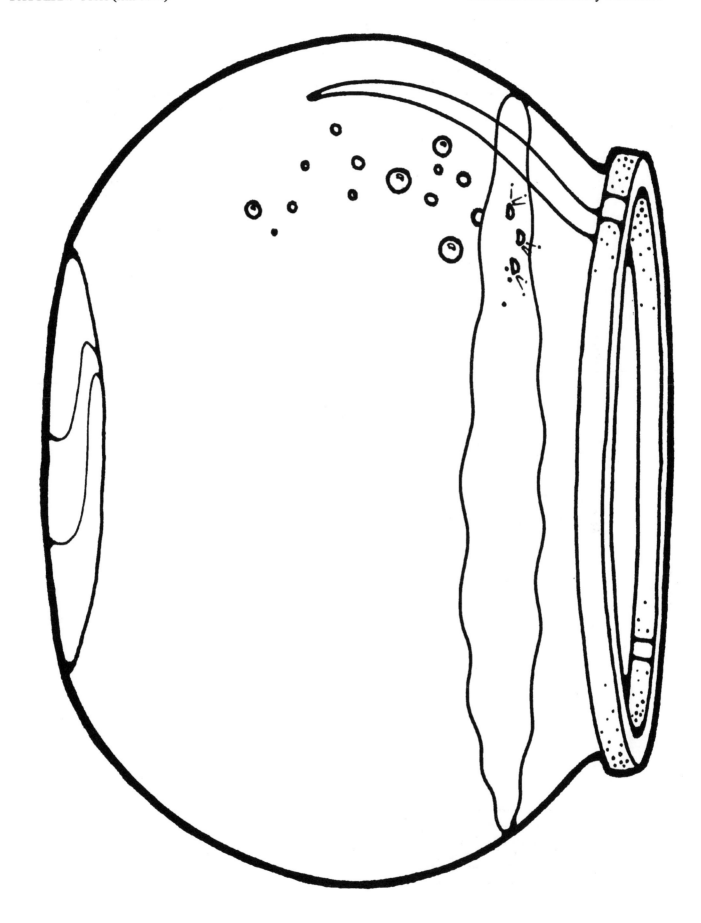

I am thankful for FOOD!

I am thankful for CLOTHES!

 *Primary 1 manual is published by The Church of Jesus Christ of Latter-day Saints, Salt Lake City, Utah.

F

FORGIVE: Jesus Wants Us to Forgive Everyone

(Joseph and brothers finger puppets)　　　　　See lesson #30 in Primary 1 manual*.

YOU'LL NEED: Copy of Joseph and brothers finger puppet patterns (page 43) on colored cardstock paper for each child, scissors, glue or tape, and crayons

ACTIVITY: Create Joseph and his brothers finger puppets to act out the story of Joseph who was sold into Egypt but forgave his brothers.
1. Color puppets.
2. Roll puppets around a pencil to curl into shape.
3. Cut out individual puppets and tape the back.
4. Slip puppets over child's fingers.

THOUGHT TREAT: Bread or crackers from grain (like the grain Joseph gave his brothers)

FRIENDS: I Can Share and Care Like Jesus

("I Can 'Bee' a Friend" friendship necklace)　　　　See lesson #33 in Primary 1 manual*.

YOU'LL NEED: Copy heart patterns (page 44) on cardstock paper, 40" of yarn or ribbon for each child, paper punch, scissors, and crayons

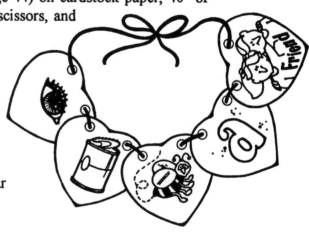

ACTIVITY: Create a necklace to show child how to be a friend like Jesus was a friend to others.
1. Color and cut out hearts.
2. Punch holes, tie yarn or ribbon through hearts, and tie at the end.
3. Place necklace around child's neck to wear home. Help them memorize verse:
"I can 'bee' a friend."

THOUGHT TREAT: Heart-shaped cookies

     *Primary 1 manual is published by The Church of Jesus Christ of Latter-day Saints, Salt Lake City, Utah.

HANDS: I Am Thankful for My Hands

(hand-some bracelet)

See lesson #17 in Primary 1 manual*.

YOU'LL NEED: Copy of hand-some bracelet patterns (page 46) on cardstock paper for each child, scissors, tape or "sticky-back" velcro, and crayons

ACTIVITY: Create a hand-some bracelet to show others you are thankful for your hands.
1. Color and cut out left and right hands.
2. Attach tape or "sticky-back" velcro to each bracelet.

THOUGHT TREAT:
Heart-or-hand-shaped sugar cookie

HELPING: I Can Help at Church

(slide show)

See lesson #44 in Primary 1 manual*.

YOU'LL NEED: Copy of church and pull-through picture strip pattern (page 47) on cardstock paper for each child, razor blade (to use prior to activity), scissors, glue, and crayons

ACTIVITY: Create a church with pull-through picture strip to show ways we can help at church.
1. Before activity, cut slits on both sides of door with a razor blade or the X-ACTO® number one knife.
2. Color and cut out the church and pull-through picture strip.
3. Slide (insert) picture strip into slits on sides of door.
4. Fold back edges of picture to prevent pulling all the way out.

THOUGHT TREAT: Chapel Door Graham Cracker Cookie (two graham crackers with frosting in the middle) When children eat, show them how to open up the sandwich like the chapel door and tell you ways they can help at church.

See lesson #17 in Primary 1 manual*.

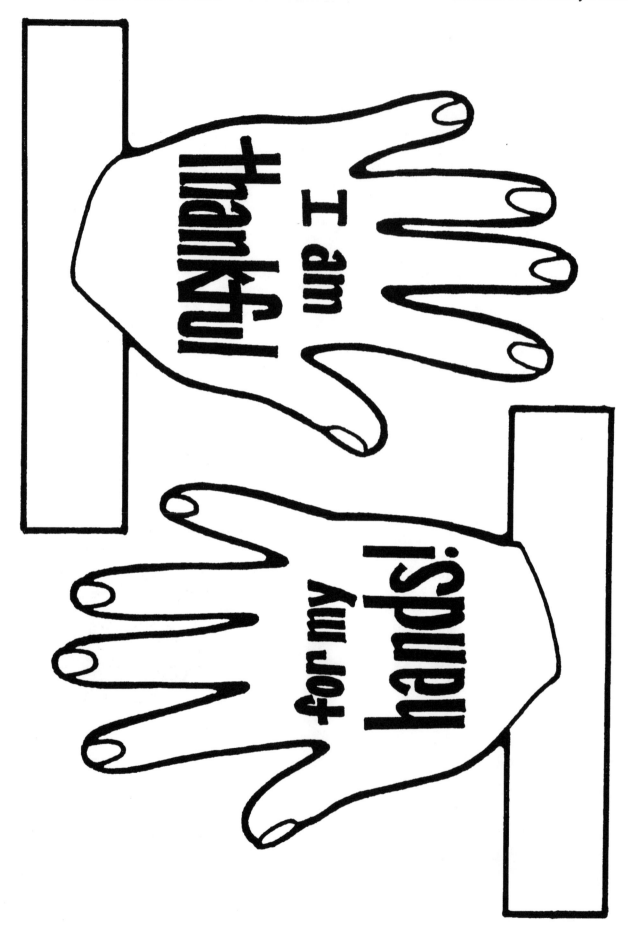

*Primary 1 manual is published by The Church of Jesus Christ of Latter-day Saints, Salt Lake City, Utah.

insert

Smile and say "Thank you"

Listen

Fold arms

Pick-up trash

Bow head

Quiet feet

I can help at church!

H

HOLY GHOST: The Holy Ghost Is My Helper

(gift package)   See lesson #7 in Primary 1 manual*.

YOU'LL NEED: Copy of gift and Holy Ghost pattern (page 49) on white cardstock paper, and a quilted or soft fabric piece for each child, glue, tape, scissors, and crayons

ACTIVITY: Create a gift package and a spirit to pull in and out of package to show that the

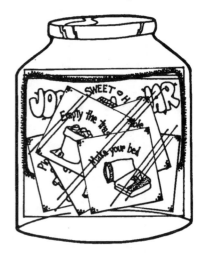

Holy Ghost is a special gift we can receive after we are baptized. Explain that the Holy Ghost does not have a body, so he can be Heavenly Father's and Jesus' helper. He can whisper the truth in our hearts and minds. He can help us make right choices. He can warn us if danger is near. He can give us a feeling of peace when we are sad. He is our comforter (show soft piece of fabric).
1. Color and cut out gift package, heart, Holy Ghost, and piece of soft fabric (comforter).
2. Fold gift package at the top and cut a slit to insert the Holy Ghost and comforter (piece of fabric).
3. Tape or glue sides and top (next to package ribbon), leaving pocket open.

THOUGHT TREAT: Heart-shaped cookie

HOME: I Am Thankful for My Home

("Home Sweet Home" job jar with jobs)   See lesson #31 in Primary 1 manual*.

YOU'LL NEED: Copies of jar and job card patterns (pages 50-51) on colored cardstock paper, a zip-close plastic sandwich bag, and six reward treats for each child, scissors, double-stick tape or glue, and crayons

ACTIVITY: To help each child feel grateful for his home. Help him/her take care of it by drawing out a job each day and doing it. With a reward treat, they will feel really neat!
1. Color and cut out job jar and job cards.
2. Attach a zip-close plastic sandwich bag to the front of jar with double-stick tape or rubber cement glue.
3. Put cards and six reward candies in bag.

THOUGHT TREAT: Reward treats--Supply six treats to place in bag. Give each child a few treats to whet their appetite for a job well done). Tell them that they are to be honest and not eat a piece of candy until one of the jobs is done. They can work each day for six days and let you know next week what they did.

The Holy Ghost can dwell in my heart. ♥

Holy Ghost has a spirit body.

The Gift of the

HOLY GHOST

Fold   Fold

The Holy Ghost will:
1. Help me know what is right.
2. Help me know that Jesus and Heavenly Father are real.
3. Give me comfort and help.

JOB HOME ∘ SWEET ∘ HOME JAR

At home I have some jobs to do,
to make the house look like new;
I will do a job each day,
With a tasty treat for pay!

*Primary 1 manual is published by The Church of Jesus Christ of Latter-day Saints, Salt Lake City, Utah.

H-J

HONESTY: I Am Happy when I Am Honest

(smile & frown hand puppet)

See lesson #37 in Primary 1 manual*.

YOU'LL NEED: Copy of puppet pattern (page 53) for each child, scissors, tape, and crayons

ACTIVITY: Create a two-sided puppet for each child to help make decisions about honesty. SMILE SIDE: Show when a choice is honest. FROWN SIDE: Show when a choice is dishonest. Read each side with children.
1. Color and cut out puppet.
2. Fold in half with smile on front and frown on back.
3. Tape outside or glue 1/4" inside on puppet top and sides, leaving the inside open for child's hand to fit in.
4. Ask children to choose which situations are honest (smile) and dishonest (frown).

THOUGHT TREAT: Smiley and Frowny Face Cookies--talk about choices as you "chews" the right cookie. As children chew on the frowny face cookie, talk about wrong choices. As they chew on the smiley face cookie, talk about right choices that make them happy.

JESUS WAS BORN: I Love the Baby Jesus

(movable manger scene)

See lesson #46 in Primary 1 manual*.

YOU'LL NEED: Copy of stable and movable picture patterns (page 54-55) on white or tan cardstock paper, zip-close plastic sandwich bag for each child, double-stick tape, scissors, and crayons

ACTIVITY: Act out the night Jesus was born by creating a manger scene with Mary, Joseph, baby Jesus, shepherds, wise men, star, and cattle.
1. Color and cut out stable and character pieces.
2. Use double-stick tape or glue to attach plastic bag to back of stable.
3. Store character pieces in bag, showing children how to act out the manger scene.

THOUGHT TREAT: Star sugar cookie

*Primary 1 manual is published by The Church of Jesus Christ of Latter-day Saints, Salt Lake City, Utah.

*Primary 1 manual is published by The Church of Jesus Christ of Latter-day Saints, Salt Lake City, Utah.

    *Primary 1 manual is published by The Church of Jesus Christ of Latter-day Saints, Salt Lake City, Utah.

See lesson #46 in Primary 1 manual*.

*Primary 1 manual is published by The Church of Jesus Christ of Latter-day Saints, Salt Lake City, Utah.

55

J-L

JESUS: Jesus Is Heavenly Father's Son

(3-D stand-up card)   See lesson #5 in Primary 1 manual*.

YOU'LL NEED: Copy of 3-D stand-up card pattern (page 57) on cardstock paper for each child, scissors, tape or glue, and crayons

ACTIVITY: Create this three-sided stand-up card to show that Jesus is Heavenly Father's Son and that Jesus obeys Heavenly Father. Tell children that when we do what is right, we are obeying Jesus and Heavenly Father. Children can say, "Jesus once was a little child like me. He learned to obey Heavenly Father and so can I."
OPTION: Teacher can complete steps 1 and 2 before class.
1. Color card.
2. Before cutting out card, fan-fold card in five places (dotted lines specify fold location).
3. Glue sides A, B, and C together to make a three-sided card.

THOUGHT TREAT: Sunshine Lollipop Cookie: Make cake mix recipe below; frost cookies white. Then, using a cake decorator tube filled with yellow frosting, make a sun.
Lollipop Cookie Recipe: One 18-ounce yellow cake mix, 3/4 cup water, and 2 eggs--Drop by tablespoons full, three inches apart, onto cookie sheet. Place wooden craft sticks into dough. Bake 8-11 minutes at 375°.
NOTE: Remind children that the sun is a special light Heavenly Father gave us to keep us warm and give us light. Jesus is also a special light. He is Heavenly Father's Son. He came to earth to help us choose the right.

LOVE: Heavenly Father and Jesus Love Me

(picture and mirror)   See lesson #6 in Primary 1 manual*.

YOU'LL NEED: Copy of two-sided picture and mirror frame pattern (page 58) on colored cardstock paper, mirror or reflective paper or heavy aluminum foil (child can see their image reflected), scissors, glue, and crayons

ACTIVITY: Talk about how Jesus loves little children. Have each child look in mirror and say, "Guess who Heavenly Father and Jesus love?" Then child can say, "Me!"
1. Color and cut out picture and mirror frame.
2. Fold in half and glue back to back.
3. Glue a mirror or foil on mirror side.

THOUGHT TREAT: Pitted olives to place on each of child's finger-tips. Explain that Heavenly Father and Jesus love us and wanted us to have a body like theirs. Heavenly Father gave us fingers like his. Let's count our fingers as we eat our olives. NOTE: Wet-wipe child's hands before and after.

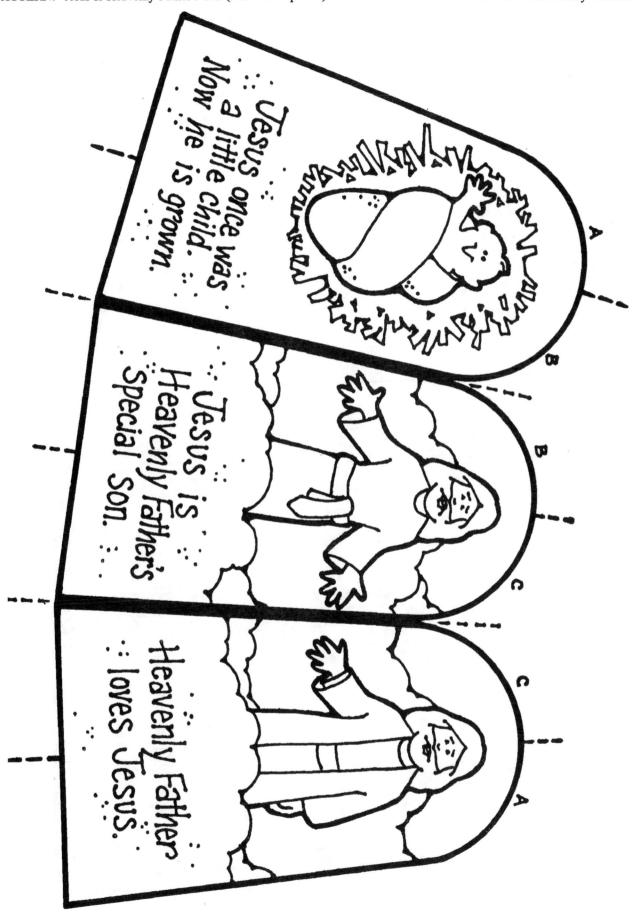

Jesus once was a little child. Now he is grown.

Jesus is Heavenly Father's Special Son.

Heavenly Father loves Jesus.

See lesson #6 in Primary 1 manual*.

Fold

Guess who Heavenly Father and Jesus love?

ME!

Heavenly Father and Jesus love the little children.

 *Primary 1 manual is published by The Church of Jesus Christ of Latter-day Saints, Salt Lake City, Utah.

L-M

LOVE OTHERS: I Can Love Others

(spiral pictures)

See lesson #34 in Primary 1 manual*.

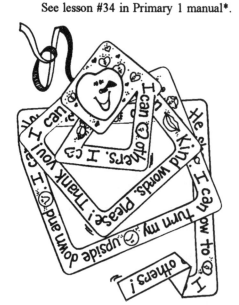

YOU'LL NEED: Copy of spiral picture pattern (page 60) on colored cardstock paper, scissors, paper punch, 6" yarn or ribbon, and crayons

ACTIVITY: Tell children they can be kind to one another by helping, saying kind words, and wearing a smile. Children will enjoy bouncing this ring of pictures. Parade them around the room to show how happy we can be when we love others.
1. Color and cut out spiral picture.
2. Punch hole at the top and tie a yarn or ribbon for child to hang item when they get home.

THOUGHT TREAT: Heart shaped cookie

MUSIC Makes Me Smile

(music charm bracelet)

See lesson #39 in Primary 1 manual*.

YOU'LL NEED: Copy of music charm patterns (page 61) on colored cardstock paper, 16" yarn or ribbon for each child, scissors, paper punch, and crayons. OPTION: Page reinforcements or tape (see #2 below)

ACTIVITY: Tell children that happy, beautiful, peaceful music can make you feel happy. It can help you think of Jesus and Heavenly Father, and be reverent in church. Ask them to pick out their favorite Primary song and sing it. Show them the notes in a music book to see where they go up and down--help them bring their voices up and down.
1. Color and cut out music bracelet charms.
2. Place page reinforcements or tape on top left corner, punch charms and thread them through yarn or ribbon.
3. Tie to child's wrist saying, "Music makes me smile."

THOUGHT TREAT: Cereal munchies threaded on charm bracelet, i.e. Cheerios®

*Primary 1 manual is published by The Church of Jesus Christ of Latter-day Saints, Salt Lake City, Utah.

PATTERN: MUSIC (music charm bracelet)   See lesson #39 in Primary 1 manual*.

O-P

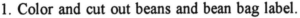

OBEDIENCE: I Have "Bean" Obedient

(bean bag)   See lesson #28 in Primary 1 manual*.

YOU'LL NEED: Copy of beans and bean family label patterns (page 63-64) on colored cardstock paper, a zip-close plastic sandwich bag for each child, scissors, and crayons

ACTIVITY: Play the "I Have 'Bean' Obedient" game with children using bean faces. Pull them out of the bag one at a time. Name the beans and ask each child how this bean has been obedient. Here's How: <u>Lova Bean</u> shows love to others, <u>Toya Bean</u> picks up toys, <u>Beda Bean</u> makes her bed, <u>Keepa Bean</u> keeps the commandments, <u>Folda Bean</u> folds his arms, <u>Whispa Bean</u> whispers in the chapel, and <u>Quiet Bean</u> walks quietly to class.
1. Color and cut out beans and bean bag label.
2. Place bean bag label inside the bag, and then the beans.

THOUGHT TREAT: Jelly Beans to place inside bag and eat in class. FUN OPTION: Glue a different colored jelly bean on each paper bean placed inside obedient bean bag.

PLAN: Heavenly Father Has a Plan for Me

(paper dolls with heavenly and earthly home)   See lesson #3 in Primary 1 manual*.

YOU'LL NEED: Copy of patterns (page 65) on colored cardstock paper, an extra 8 1/2" x 11" sheet of cardstock paper for mounting (per child), several plastic notebook sheets (to make spirit) for each child, scissors, and crayons. NOTE: One sheet of plastic can cut out three or four spirit dolls.

ACTIVITY: Create a heavenly and earthly home, a plastic spirit, and a paper doll to show how the spirit is without the body in heaven and goes into the body when it comes to earth. When we die, the body stays on earth and the spirit goes back to heaven.
1. Color and cut out heavenly and earthly homes and paper doll (boy or girl).
2. Fold heavenly and earthly homes lengthwise and cut slits for pockets to enclose paper doll and plastic spirit.
3. Glue-mount heavenly home at the top and earthly home at the bottom on the extra 8 1/2" x 11" sheet of cardstock paper. HOW TO MOUNT: Glue sides, top and bottom 1/4" inch, leaving center open for pocket.
4. Cut out plastic doll using paper doll pattern (cut head on fold line). Plastic spirit should have two sides to slip over paper doll when showing how spirit enters and leaves the body.

THOUGHT TREATS: HEAVEN & EARTH COOKIE: Frost cookie with white clouds on top and chocolate earth on bottom. HEAVEN & EARTH PUDDING ART: Form a cloud and earth with vanilla and chocolate pudding on waxed paper, then eat the pudding picture.

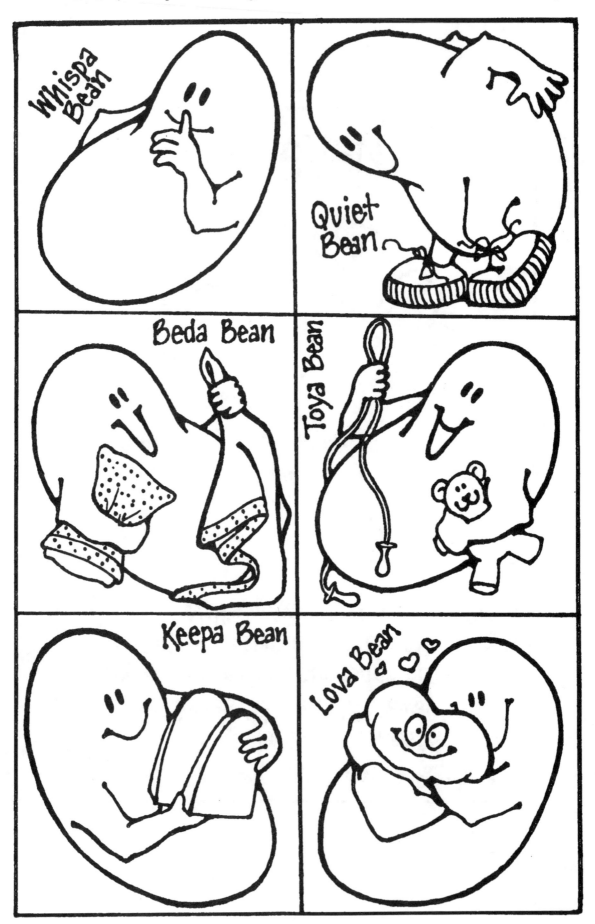

 *Primary 1 manual is published by The Church of Jesus Christ of Latter-day Saints, Salt Lake City, Utah.

I am Heavenly Father's spirit child.

I came to earth for a body.

P

PRAY: To Heavenly Father I Will Pray

(Daniel and lions' den drama scene)

See lesson #4 in Primary 1 manual*.

YOU'LL NEED: Copy Daniel, den, and lions patterns (page 67) on tan cardstock paper for each child, scissors, and crayons

ACTIVITY: Create Daniel and lions' den to help children act out the scene where Daniel prayed to Heavenly Father. Then the lions did not eat Daniel. READ: Daniel 6.

THOUGHT TREAT: Cream Filled Cookies or Crackers. Say, "These cookies or crackers are like our hands in prayer. They come together and are folded and quiet. Then when the prayer is over, they can unfold. After the prayer is over, let's remember to keep our hands still. Keep your hands folded or in your lap. This is being reverent in Heavenly Father's house."

PRAYER: I Like to Pray with My Family

(family prayer fan)

See lesson #27 in Primary 1 manual*.

YOU'LL NEED: Copy of fan pattern (page 68) on colored lightweight paper for each child, yarn or ribbon, scissors, paper punch, and crayons

ACTIVITY: Create a family prayer fan to show children that Heavenly Father wants us to pray with our family every day. You will receive many blessings as you pray with your family.
1. Color and cut out fan.
2. Fan-fold paper into a fan.
3. Punch a hole at the bottom of the fan and tie yarn or ribbon through hole to hold fan together.

THOUGHT TREAT: Fan-tastic Cookie (shape cookie dough in fan shape, cut lines in cookie and bake). COLORFUL OPTION: Mix food coloring with 1 teaspoon canned milk (use primary colors: red, yellow, and blue) and paint lines in cookie before baking.

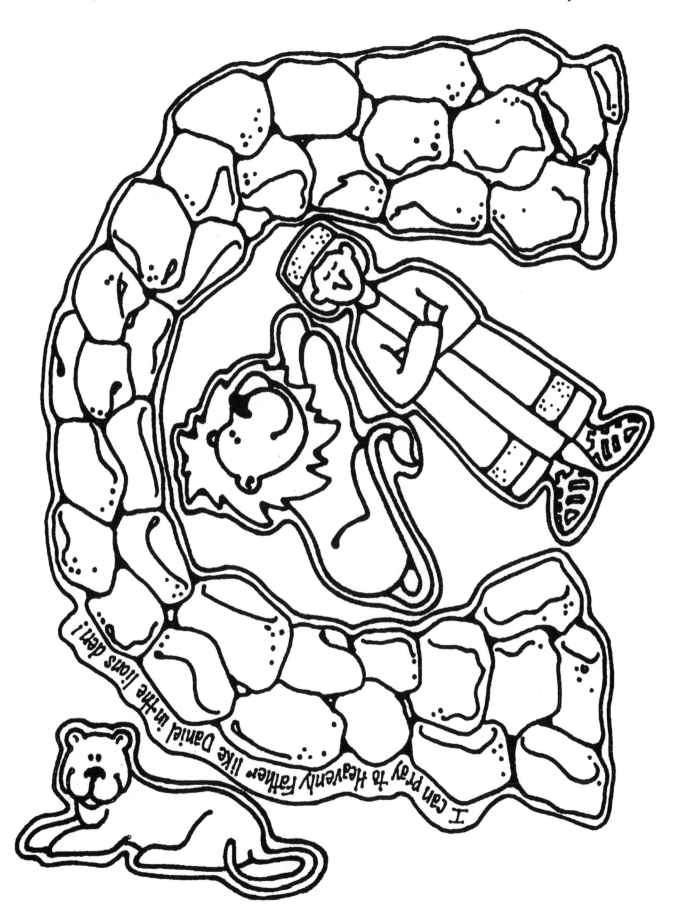

I can pray to Heavenly Father like Daniel in the lions' den!

PROPHET: I Know the Prophet Lives

(prophet poster or fold-out pictures)

See lesson #43 in Primary 1 manual*.

YOU'LL NEED: Copy of fold-out picture patterns (page 70) on colored lightweight paper for each child, scissors, glue or tape and crayons

ACTIVITY: Create a fold-out poster showing pictures of prophets who talk to Heavenly Father and Jesus. Let children know they are blessed when they follow the prophet.
1. Color and cut out picture strips.
2. Tape or glue part B to the bottom of part A where indicated.
3. Fold on middle line. Then fan-fold part A and B to create a set of fold-out pictures. Child can take home to post on wall.

THOUGHT TREAT: Prophet Punch. In small cups, pour each child some punch and say: "The prophet brings us many blessings. As we sip our punch, let's think of each prophet we have learned about and tell about him."

REVERENCE Begins with Me

(church mouse maze)

See lesson #38 in Primary 1 manual*.

YOU'LL NEED: Copy of church mouse maze and church mouse pattern (page 71) on colored cardstock paper for each child, scissors, and crayons

ACTIVITY: Create and go through church mouse maze to show children how to be reverent in each room of the church house. When they are reverent in Heavenly Father's house, they are showing love to him and to Jesus.
1. Color and cut out maze and mouse.
2. Move mouse through the front door and into the rooms, talking about reverence.
3. Tape mouse to maze for child to take home.

THOUGHT TREAT: Cookie church house
(cut out sugar cookie dough in church house shape and bake 350° for 8-10 minutes)
OPTION: Before baking, press licorice rope in dough for steeple, windows, and door.

S

SABBATH DAY: Sunday Is My Best Day

(creation collar)   See lesson #15 in Primary 1 manual*.

YOU'LL NEED: Copy of collar patterns part A and B
(pages 73-74) on colored cardstock paper for each child, tape or glue, scissors, and crayons

ACTIVITY: Create a creation collar to show the six days of creation and the seventh day of rest.

1. Color and cut out parts A and B.
2. Glue or tape parts A and B together.
3. Place around child's neck.

THOUGHT TREAT: Day 7 Cookie (cut out sugar cookies in the shape of a "7" for the seventh day of creation or an "S" for Sabbath or Sunday, and bake). Children may have fun frosting the cookie and decorating with colored candies.

QUICK-TO-MAKE OPTION: Make pancakes in days 1-7 shapes. Top with honey butter (mix 1/4 part honey with 3/4 part butter or peanut butter).

SACRAMENT: I Like to Remember Jesus

(sacrament manners match game)   See lesson #40 in Primary 1 manual*.

YOU'LL NEED: Two copies of match game cards (page 75) on colored cardstock paper for each child to take home and one set to play with in class, scissors, and crayons

ACTIVITY: Assemble a match game for each child and place in an envelope or zip-close plastic sandwich bag to remind them of how they should act during the sacrament.
        COLOR AND CUT OUT CARD SETS.
TO PLAY: Turn cards face down. Take turns turning two cards over to try and make a match. If cards match, keep matching cards. If cards don't match, turn cards back over and next player tries to make a match.
SACRAMENT HOW TO: Show sacrament cups with water and bread. Show how to pick up the bread and pass it on, and to drink the water and return the cup to the tray (don't actually eat food).

THOUGHT TREAT: Cookies or graham crackers

*Primary 1 manual is published by The Church of Jesus Christ of Latter-day Saints, Salt Lake City, Utah.

PART A

*Primary 1 manual is published by The Church of Jesus Christ of Latter-day Saints, Salt Lake City, Utah.

S

SCRIPTURES: From Heavenly Father and Jesus

(scripture specs)

See lesson #41 in Primary 1 manual*.

YOU'LL NEED: Copy of scripture specs (eye glasses) pattern (page 77) on colored cardstock paper and a bible (with John 5:39 marked) for each child, glue or tape, paper punch, 30" yarn or elastic string, scissors, and crayons. OPTION: colored cellophane

ACTIVITY: Create some scripture specs to make scripture reading fun. Have children put them on as you help them read from the scriptures (John 5:39). Explain that "testify" means tell. The scriptures tell us about Jesus and Heavenly Father.
1. Color and cut out specs. Cut out center of specs ahead of time with a razor blade.
2. Punch holes in sides.
3. Tie yarn or elastic string through holes.
4. Tie behind child's head over ears.
COLORFUL OPTION: Glue colored cellophane on the inside of glasses to see through, i.e. rose or blue colored glasses.

THOUGHT TREAT: Cookie Scripture Book (cut sugar cookie dough into book shape and frost). OPTION: Top with rectangular shaped wafer cookies.

SMELL & TASTE: I Am Thankful For

(giant nose and tongue mask)

See lesson #20 in Primary 1 manual*.

YOU'LL NEED: Copy of nose and tongue mask pattern (page 78) on flesh-colored cardstock paper, and 30" of yarn or elastic string for each child, paper punch, scissors, and crayons

ACTIVITY: Create a giant nose and tongue child can wear home to show they are thankful they can smell and taste.
1. Color and cut out mask.
2. Fold mask in half lengthwise and cut out nose and mouth (to fit over child's face).
3. Punch a hole and tie yarn or elastic string on each end. Tie behind child's head over ears.

THOUGHT TREAT: Foods that smell and taste good

*Primary 1 manual is published by The Church of Jesus Christ of Latter-day Saints, Salt Lake City, Utah.

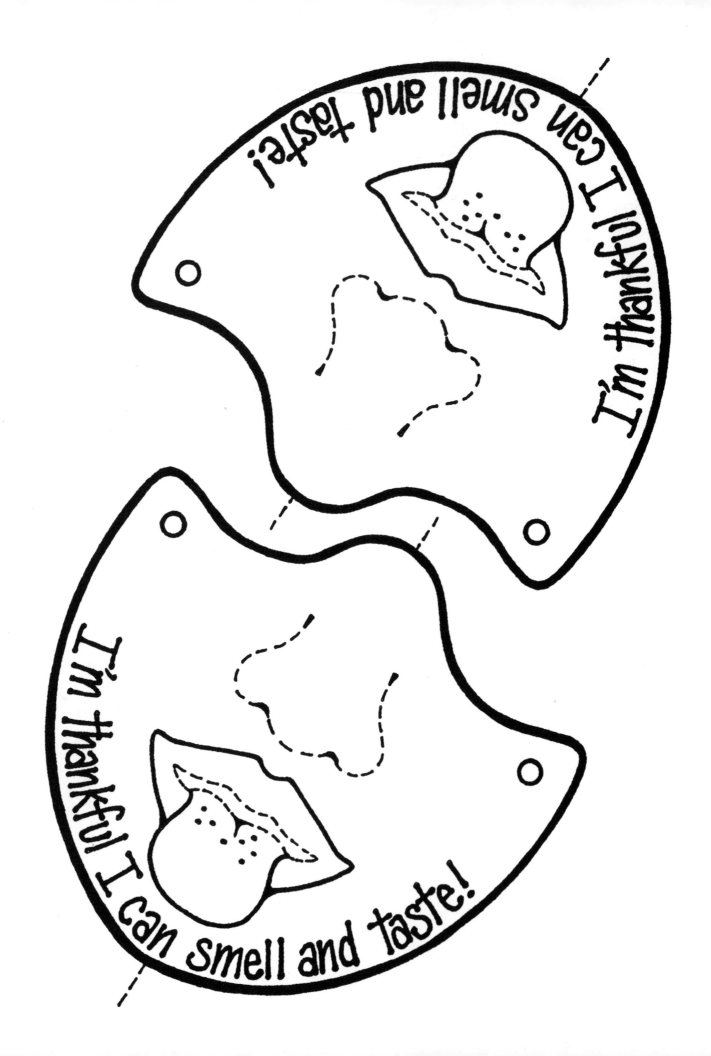

SORRY: I Can Say Hippopotamus. I Can Say I'm Sorry.

(hippo sack puppet)

See lesson #29 in Primary 1 manual*.

YOU'LL NEED: Copy hippo puppet pattern (page 80) on brown or gray cardstock paper, small lunch sack for each child, glue, scissors, and crayons

ACTIVITY: Children can enjoy saying "I'm sorry" with their hippo sack puppet. With the sack, rehearse the word hippopotamus. If they can say this big word, they can say "I'm sorry" when they do something wrong.
1. Color and cut out hippo face.
2. Glue hippo head on bottom of sack, and jaw in the middle of the sack. When fingers move sack flap up and down, hippo's mouth opens wide as child says "I'm sorry."

THOUGHT TREAT: Animal crackers or cookies (Look for the hippos!)

THINGS: I Can Do Many Things

(shirt with giant buttons--sewing card)

See lesson #22 in Primary 1 manual*.

YOU'LL NEED: Copy of shirt pattern (page 81) on colored cardstock paper for each child, tape, scissors, 16" yarn or ribbon, paper punch, and crayons

ACTIVITY: Let the child actually show you and the family they can do something special. Let them create a shirt and pretend to sew on buttons to proudly take home.
1. Color and cut out shirt sewing card.
2. Fold shirt in half and punch holes in shirt where indicated.
3. Thread (sew) yarn or ribbon through buttons (start sewing from underneath shirt sewing card).
4. Loosely tie yarn or ribbon together in a bow, or tape to inside of shirt sewing card so child can sew again.

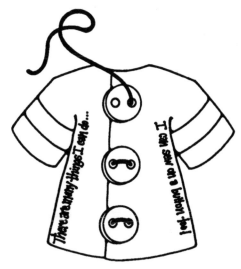

THOUGHT TREAT: Big Button Cookies: Frost a round cookie and place two round candies or chocolate chips (upside down) in the center to look like button holes.

*Primary 1 manual is published by The Church of Jesus Christ of Latter-day Saints, Salt Lake City, Utah.

79

If I can say

Hippopotamus

I can say

I'm Sorry!

*Primary 1 manual is published by The Church of Jesus Christ of Latter-day Saints, Salt Lake City, Utah.

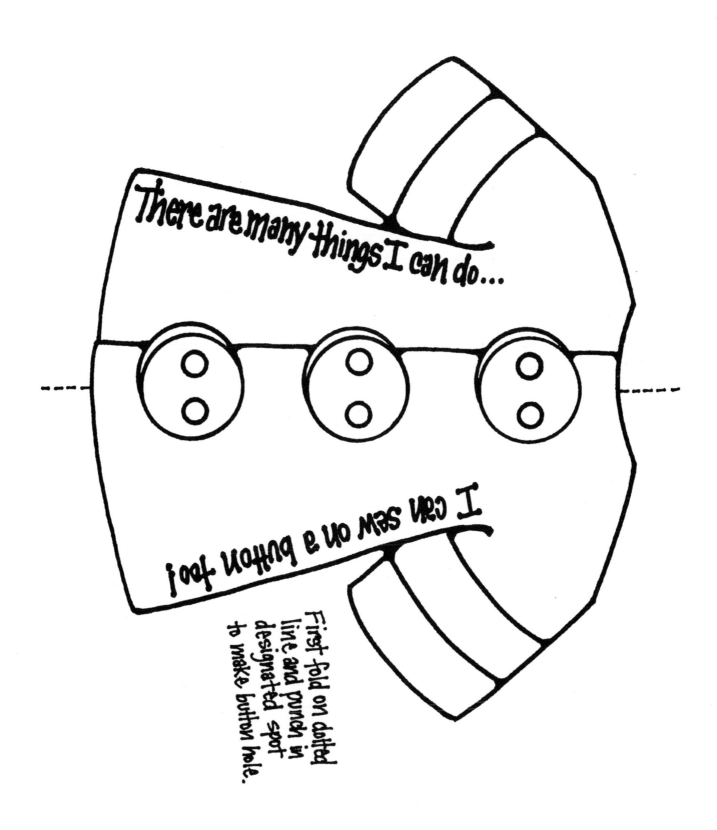

There are many things I can do...

I can sew on a button too!

First fold on dotted line and punch in designated spot to make button hole.

TREES, PLANTS & FLOWERS: Heavenly Father's Garden

(bracelets or binoculars)

See lesson #10 in Primary 1 manual*.

YOU'LL NEED: Copy a set of bracelets (page 83) on light green cardstock paper for each child, scissors, glue or tape, and crayons

ACTIVITY: Create a triangle shape that children can use to learn about trees, plants, and flowers. Children love to use these as bracelets, slipping them over their little hands. They like to look through them like binoculars, looking up and down and all around the room. They look at nature, the teacher, and the other children through these fun triangular shapes.
1. Color and cut out triangle.
2. Glue and then tape together to reinforce, allowing time to dry.

THOUGHT TREAT: Eatable plants, i.e. apples, carrots, celery, or broccoli. Children like to call broccoli "trees."

WATER: It's a Wonder

(umbrella picture with raindrop glue-on stickers)

See lesson #9 in Primary 1 manual*.

YOU'LL NEED: Copy patterns (page 84) on colored cardstock paper for each child, scissors, glue, and crayons

ACTIVITY: Create a raindrop picture to show how grateful we feel for water. Remind children to thank Heavenly Father and Jesus for this wonderful creation.
1. Color and cut umbrella picture and raindrops.
2. Glue raindrops on picture.
3. Children can say: "Drip, drop, the rain drops, falling on the ground," as they make this wonderful water picture.

THOUGHT TREAT: Cake Raindrop Cookies: Mix an 18-oz. white or yellow cake mix with 3/4 cup water and 2 eggs. Drop on a cookie sheet by tablespoons full (drag batter to raindrop point). Bake 350° for 8-10 minutes. OPTION: Color batter light blue to look like water with the blue sky's reflection (reduce the amount of water 1/2 to 1 teaspoon).

      *Primary 1 manual is published by The Church of Jesus Christ of Latter-day Saints, Salt Lake City, Utah.

PATTERN: TREES, PLANTS, & FLOWERS (triangle bracelet/binoculars)   See lesson #10 in Primary 1 manual*.

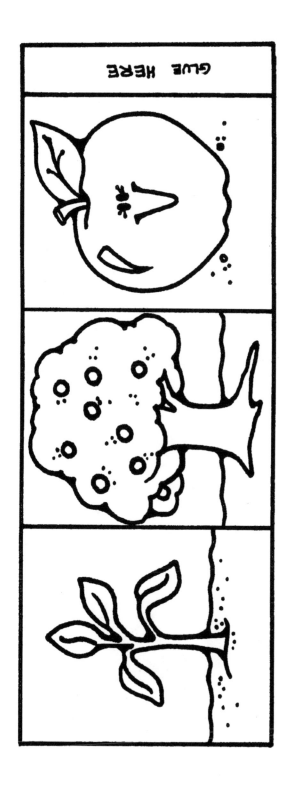

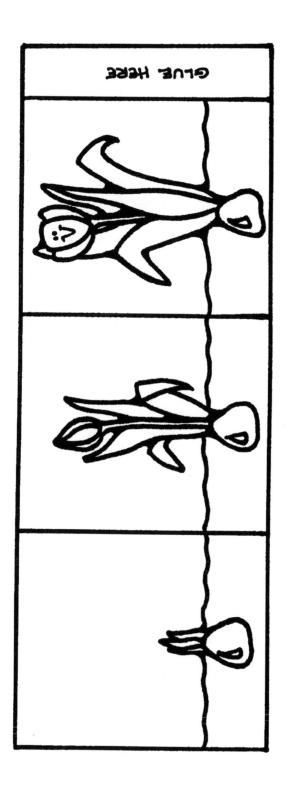

PATTERN: WATER (umbrella picture with raindrop glue-on stickers)   See lesson #9 in Primary 1 manual*.

     *Primary 1 manual is published by The Church of Jesus Christ of Latter-day Saints, Salt Lake City, Utah.

MARY H. ROSS, Author

Mary Ross is an energetic mother and Primary teacher who loves to help children have a good time while they learn. She is a published author and columnist and has studied acting, modeling, and voice. Her varied interests include writing, creating activities, children's parties, and cooking. Mary and her husband Paul live with their daughter Jennifer in Sandy, Utah.

Photos by Scott Hancock, Provo, Utah.

JENNETTE GUYMON, Illustrator

Jennette has studied graphic arts and illustration at Utah Valley State College and the University of Utah, and is currently employed with a commercial construction company. She served a mission to Japan and enjoys languages, sports, reading, cooking, art, and freelance illustrating. Jennette lives in Salt Lake City, Utah, and attends the Mount Olympus Third Ward.

Mary Ross, Author and Jennette Guymon, Illustrator are creators of the series
**"Search, Ponder and Play:
SUPER SCRIPTURE ACTIVITIES."**
Books include activities for family home evenings, Primary sharing time, classroom activities, talks, and more.
Inside You'll Find:

○ Search & Ponder cards to find missing words and ponder gospel questions
○ Scripture Show & Tell presentations with pictures to color with cue-cards
○ Games or activities to make learning fun,
○ Songs from the Primary Children's Songbook
○ Favor and prize patterns--ready to copy, cut and paste
○ Thought Treats to sweeten the appetite for scripture reading
○ And more!